Many thanks
Melissa Castan

IN THE NATIONAL INTEREST

General Sir John Monash once exhorted a graduating class to 'equip yourself for life, not solely for your own benefit but for the benefit of the whole community'. At the university established in his name, we repeat this statement to our own graduating classes, to acknowledge how important it is that common or public good flows from education.

Universities spread and build on the knowledge they acquire through scholarship in many ways, well beyond the transmission of this learning through education. It is a necessary part of a university's role to debate its findings, not only with other researchers and scholars, but also with the broader community in which it resides.

Publishing for the benefit of society is an important part of a university's commitment to free intellectual inquiry. A university provides civil space for such inquiry by its scholars, as well as for investigations by public intellectuals and expert practitioners.

This series, In the National Interest, embodies Monash University's mission to extend knowledge and encourage informed debate about matters of great significance to Australia's future.

Professor Margaret Gardner AC
President and Vice-Chancellor,
Monash University

MELISSA CASTAN &
LYNETTE RUSSELL

TIME TO LISTEN: AN INDIGENOUS VOICE TO PARLIAMENT

Time to Listen: An Indigenous Voice to Parliament

Monash University Publishing
Matheson Library Annexe
40 Exhibition Walk
Monash University
Clayton, Victoria 3800, Australia
https://publishing.monash.edu

Monash University Publishing brings to the world publications which advance the best traditions of humane and enlightened thought.

ISBN: 9781922979124 (paperback)
ISBN: 9781922979148 (ebook)

Series: In the National Interest
Editor: Greg Bain
Project manager & copyeditor: Paul Smitz
Designer: Peter Long
Typesetter: Cannon Typesetting
Proofreader: Gillian Armitage
Printed in Australia by Ligare Book Printers

A catalogue record for this book is available from the National Library of Australia.

The paper this book is printed on is in accordance with the standards of the Forest Stewardship Council®. The FSC® promotes environmentally responsible, socially beneficial and economically viable management of the world's forests.

We dedicate this book both to our ancestors, acknowledging their journeys and struggles of the past, and to our children, who will continue our journeys into the future. And to the countless generations who have gone before us, who were never listened to, we hear you now. We are listening.

AUTHORS' NOTE

We write as academics whose research interests include the history of and laws affecting First Nations peoples. We have worked together for over twenty years, and during this time we have come to a mutual understanding of how history influences law and how law itself is historical. In Lynette Russell's case, she writes as a historian, and although hers too is an Aboriginal viewpoint, it must be emphasised that it is merely one of a multitude. Melissa Castan writes as a legal scholar concerned with the features and flaws of the Anglo-Australian legal system. We do not purport to speak for First Nations peoples. Instead, we are concerned with the capacity of the law to deliver justice for First Nations peoples and to rebalance the systemic inequities they face across all areas of society.

Indigenous is a term used to describe First Nations peoples around the world generally. In Australia, it is used to indicate Aboriginal and Torres Strait Islander peoples specifically. We prefer to use 'First Nations' or 'First Peoples', unless specific community names are appropriate, such as the Wurundjeri, Bunurong, Yorta Yorta and so on. We have also adopted a somewhat conventional Western use of terms such as 'international law', 'sovereignty' and 'nation'. We certainly acknowledge that these terms and the political–legal assumptions underpinning them are contested and not accepted by some Indigenous people.

We also note that the debate around the Voice has moved quickly, and will continue to do so. This piece was written in the first half of 2023, and was accurate at the time of writing.

~

It is traditional within Indigenous culture that you introduce yourself proper way; that is, where you come from both literally and philosophically. With that in mind, we offer some personal insights and histories as context for the ideas and opinions that follow.

Lynette Russell

I grew up in Melbourne's outer suburbs. Most weekends, my father, grandfather and, briefly, my great-grandfather would go fishing or rabbit hunting. They often brought mushrooms home with them. I was rarely permitted to go with them. One weekend, I had my first taste of black wattle sap, which had been collected straight from the tree. I was unaware at the time that I was seeing information that had been passed down through the centuries from the mother of my Aboriginal grandmother's mother, and shared with husbands and children.

At first, I slowly gained an awareness of Aboriginal culture, but over the last forty years I have committed myself to knowing as much as I can. I pursued a PhD at the University of Melbourne in the mid-1990s after studying history, archaeology, anthropology and ethnography out of a thirst for knowledge. My doctoral research examined how Aboriginal people had been portrayed in scholarly and popular works up to the European Bicentenary in 1988. I realised that tribal, group and regional diversity had mainly been disregarded or forgotten, with Aboriginal people and culture homogenised in most cases. My first academic works were designed to underline the importance of identifying regional and cultural differences, to demonstrate the incredible variety that has resulted from a continent with more than 600 distinct 'tribes' and over 250 different languages.[1]

In 1996 I began working with the Victorian Native Title Unit. Previously, I had worked at Aboriginal Affairs Victoria, in the Victoria Archaeological Survey, where I became immersed in the Victorian Koori community—friendships and relationships were formed that have lasted ever since. However, it has been less the academic work and more the hands-on community engagement, and what I call Country work, that has genuinely educated me. Respected Wotjobaluk Elder Uncle Jack Kennedy took the time to teach me how to listen, see and feel out in the desert of western Victoria. Having known my great-grandmother, he and his brother, Uncle Patrick, took me to some of the sites that were significant in her life but that our family had forgotten over time.

Historians generally rely on written sources, and occasionally oral testimony. To tell the stories of the past, I use any hints I may find in my toolkit—texts, musical compositions, objects, archaeology—which is why I describe myself as an anthropological historian. I can piece together additional information for each skerrick of evidence to create a more detailed picture of the past. I've had a lot of successful research partnerships because of this kind of interdisciplinary history writing. Interdisciplinary history, such as we present here in this book, is often much more than the sum of its parts.

Melissa Castan

My parents' families were 'new Australians', immigrants from Eastern Europe who wanted to start fresh lives in what they were told was a 'new nation'. My mother, Nellie, was born in Kazakhstan after her parents, Nina and Jerry, left Warsaw on the eve of World War II and travelled through Soviet Russia. After the war, they discovered that, except for one sister, their parents, brothers and cousins had all been murdered. The family lived in 'Displaced Persons' camps until 1951, when they were granted visas to Australia.

My father Ron Castan's family arrived in Australia from Ukraine in 1927, fleeing pogroms, starvation and poverty. Ron was the first of his family to go to university, and he became a barrister in the mid-1960s. Driven by a strong commitment to social justice, he worked on several cases, the most notable of which was *Mabo*, named after lead plaintiff Eddie Koiki Mabo. In that 1992 case, the High Court found that previous expressions of Australian law had been wrong: Indigenous land title was capable of being recognised within the Australian legal framework. This was not a doctrine imagined by judges acting beyond their remit. It accorded with the law that had long been accepted in other British colonies.

Mabo formed the foundation for my own pathway into a career in legal education. During a prolonged break from university studies in 1989, I worked, with my partner Robert, as a legal intern on the *Mabo* case, in hearings before Justice Moynihan in Queensland. We supported the plaintiff's legal team of Ron Castan, Bryan Keon-Cohen and Greg McIntyre, assisting with historical research, taking evidentiary statements from Islander witnesses, and arranging logistics such as travel from the Torres Strait to Brisbane, where the court was determining 'findings of fact' in order that the case before the High Court could proceed. After that work concluded, I completed my law degree and graduated at Monash University.

The work and knowledge I had contributed, if only in a small way, to the outcome of a landmark Australian case shifted my understanding of what studying, practising and educating in law could mean. Now I am a legal academic who has been working in the realm of human rights, public and constitutional law for nearly thirty years. My formative experience working with Torres Strait Islanders and their legal advocates set my course. I am focused on opportunities to educate on the recognition and implementation of proper legal relations with First Nations peoples and the advancement of social justice through law reform and legal education in Australia. I have closely followed the Uluru Dialogues and seek to respond meaningfully to the invitation within the Uluru Statement from the Heart.

TIME TO LISTEN: AN INDIGENOUS VOICE TO PARLIAMENT

In March 2023, Dr Mary Graham, Kombu-merri and Waka Waka philosopher, observed in the Coral Bell School Inaugural Annual Lecture on Indigenous Diplomacy at the Australian National University in Canberra, that the Australian nation has exercised power through invasion, while Aboriginal people have always had authority, even when they have been relatively powerless. In a plea for a reconciled and fair Australia, Dr Graham asserted that we must embrace Indigenous connections in politics, polities and ways of being. She argued that to develop a proper sense of history in Australia, we must not only come to terms with its founding violence, but also engage with Indigenous people as political interlocutors—in short to hear, to listen, and to reject the silence.

In this book, we historicise and contextualise the request to be heard that Aboriginal and Torres Strait Islander peoples have made since the earliest days of colonisation. It is now manifest through the invitation issued in the Uluru Statement from the Heart, and the proposal to alter the Constitution to recognise the First Peoples of Australia by establishing an Aboriginal and Torres Strait Islander Voice, on which there is to be a national referendum late in 2023.

The Indigenous Voice to Parliament represents a call for a new formal political mechanism for Indigenous people in Australia to have input into the decisions and policies that affect them. The aim of the proposal is to develop an advisory body in such a way as to address the historical marginalisation and continuing challenges faced by Indigenous communities, by providing an ongoing platform for them to voice their concerns, aspirations and priorities in the development of national laws and policies. The Voice is intended to bring Indigenous perspectives to the foreground of the Australian political landscape.

The concept of an Indigenous Voice to Parliament entered the public spotlight with the 2017 Uluru Statement, which itself was the outcome of a series of nationwide consultations with Indigenous communities. The statement called for the creation of a First Nations Voice enshrined in the Australian Constitution to advise parliament on matters related to Indigenous affairs. It also called for a Makarrata Commission, to develop agreement-making and truth-telling as a form of transitional justice.

The Voice will be a representative body composed of Indigenous people drawn from a wide variety of communities. As such, the proposal is for a mere advisory body providing representations and perspectives on legislation, policies and programs that affect Indigenous people. This mechanism aims to ensure that Indigenous voices are heard, respected and given appropriate weight in the decision-making process. It will not be a federal department. It will not make law. Nor will it fund policies and programs.

This is a modest but crucial step towards Indigenous self-determination and advancing reconciliation. By giving Indigenous communities a formal role in shaping policies and programs, the Voice will acknowledge the right of Indigenous people to participate in matters that directly affect them. This is its essence: self-determination. It will not preclude other institutions, platforms or roles for Indigenous advocacy. The Voice will play more than a symbolic role of recognition. It is a step forward in substantive inclusion and recognition, bridging the gap between the dominant political system and Indigenous people in order to foster a stronger sense of inclusion, representation and ownership concerning decisions that impact their lives.

The Voice will work to uphold parliamentary supremacy and the effective operation of the executive government, and crucially, it will allow the nation to meet its commitments under international human rights law. As Professor Tom Calma and Professor Marcia Langton, two highly respected and experienced leaders, clearly articulated in their 2021 *Indigenous Voice Discussion Paper*:

> A National Voice would be a small national body of Aboriginal and Torres Strait Islander members providing advice to the Australian Parliament and Government. A National Voice would provide the mechanism to ensure that Aboriginal and Torres Strait Islander people have a direct say on legislation and policies that affect them.

Understanding the emergence of the Uluru Statement and the Voice to Parliament at this moment in time requires an appreciation of the journey we have taken to arrive here. This historical background is necessary to appreciate what justices Deane and

Gaudron described as 'a history of unutterable shame' in their *Mabo* judgment, and what the Uluru Statement described as 'the torment of our powerlessness'. We will then take a closer look at the nature of the representative advisory body known as the Voice and the reason for holding a referendum to amend the Australian Constitution. And we will profile many Indigenous voices as we explore the meaning and significance of the Voice.

First, we set out here the opening words of the Uluru Statement from the Heart:

> We, gathered at the 2017 National Constitutional Convention, coming from all points of the southern sky, make this statement from the heart: Our Aboriginal and Torres Strait Islander tribes were the first sovereign Nations of the Australian continent and its adjacent islands, and possessed it under our own laws and customs.
>
> This our ancestors did, according to the reckoning of our culture, from the Creation, according to the common law from 'time immemorial', and according to science more than 60 000 years ago.
>
> This sovereignty is a spiritual notion: the ancestral tie between the land, or 'mother nature', and the Aboriginal and Torres Strait Islander peoples

> who were born therefrom, remain attached thereto, and must one day return thither to be united with our ancestors.
>
> This link is the basis of the ownership of the soil, or better, of sovereignty. It has never been ceded or extinguished, and co-exists with the sovereignty of the Crown. How could it be otherwise? That peoples possessed a land for sixty millennia and this sacred link disappears from world history in merely the last two hundred years?
>
> With substantive constitutional change and structural reform, we believe this ancient sovereignty can shine through as a fuller expression of Australia's nationhood.[2]

We believe that the Uluru Statement and the Voice to Parliament should be seen as the most recent—and we hope final—request to be heard and listened to, in a long history of claims for recognition and substantive engagement. It is not, we argue, a mere political moment in time.

LISTENING TO HISTORY

In 1968, the anthropologist WEH Stanner discussed the 'cult of forgetfulness' practised on a national scale in Australia in his Boyer lectures entitled *After the Dreaming*. He dubbed this the 'Great Australian Silence'. This was a silence in which non-Indigenous Australians not only refused to acknowledge the brutality of colonialism and the disease, massacre and dispossession that accompanied it, but also chose not to think about First Nations peoples at all. From this perspective, the 'cult' was an intentional effort by non-Indigenous Australians to disregard or forget the history and accomplishments of Indigenous Australians, as well as to stifle any viewpoints that ran counter to the widely held narrative of heroic pioneers taming a savage land and creating a modern nation. This deliberate forgetting was sustained for generations, dominating the first half of the twentieth century. So persuasive was it that the historian Henry Reynolds was moved to entitle one of his books with the oft-repeated cry of 'Why weren't we told?'.

Stanner's silence was both structural and literal. For much of the last 200 or so years, popular depictions of Australian First Nations peoples were filled with negative stereotypes. We won't do so, but we could easily remind the reader of these, particularly as many have become prominent again as we debate the Voice to Parliament. The continuous marginalisation and systemic discrimination of First Nations peoples in Australia were underpinned by these stereotypes and misconceptions.

The wilful ignorance of history and an unquestioned belief in the concept of a 'fair go' for everyone, according to Stanner, were key characteristics of this cult of silence. Stanner even went as far as to suggest that institutions and sectors including education, the media and public policy actively promoted the national amnesia. Although it can be asserted that the silence has essentially been broken over the past half-century, it has not completely been replaced by a 'cult of listening'. What Stanner carefully articulated was the schism that runs through Australian society, particularly in relation to the twentieth century—a schism that marked a significant and enduring fault line.

~

In 1768, Lieutenant James Cook, captain of the bark *Endeavour*, master navigator and cartographer, began the first of his three South Pacific voyages (1768–79). On each passage, Cook carried 'Secret Instructions' from the British admiralty. His initial expedition was to ascertain whether the 'Continent or Land of Great Extent' that some said existed in the Southern

Hemisphere was real or not. Cook was specifically ordered, 'with the Consent of the Natives', to 'take possession of Convenient Situations in the Country in the Name of the King of Great Britain'.[3]

The admiralty's secret orders represent the first English statement of legal interest in the territory that would come to be known as Australia. They record the British quest for scientific discovery and exploitable resources, and the expansion of its control of strategic trading posts around the globe. They represent the colonial enterprise and probably the first expression of Anglo-Australian public law. Of course, Cook did not 'discover' Australia; at best, he mapped the east coast. He did claim possession of New South Wales, as the entire east coast of the continent was then known. However, contrary to the admiralty's instructions, this claim was not made with the consent of any of the Indigenous nations that populated the region.

Cook died almost a decade before governor Arthur Phillip arrived to establish a penal colony at Botany Bay, later Port Jackson. Phillip and his contemporaries assumed they had legal possession of the lands and waters of the Australian continent. These claims showed little concern for proper legal relations with any of the hundreds of different tribal nations that had had both legal and functional sovereignty for tens of thousands of years. Cook did not see the complex kinship networks, the social rules, rights and obligations that controlled peoples' lives. He saw neither ownership nor law.

This created a deep fracture, or fault line, in Australian law, at first politely described as a legal fiction but which later commentators referred to as terra nullius. This was an imagined state that removed Indigenous people from the land, allowing the British to assume for all practical purposes that Australia was unoccupied before Cook and Phillip staked their claims. The claims to the territory did not meet the standards set by the British, nor did they meet contemporary standards, legal or otherwise. They differed markedly from the way in which British settler colonialism played out in North America and Aotearoa/New Zealand, where treaties were sought—though usually later dishonoured. Basically, if Australia was deemed to be terra nullius, there was simply no requirement for a treaty or agreement.

Unlike Cook's observations, or perhaps his failure to observe, governor Phillip, through his close, complex and at times fraught relationship with Eora warrior Bennelong, would have been aware of Indigenous connections to land. He was, furthermore, cognisant of his obligations to Indigenous people as a colonial official. When Phillip arranged for Bennelong and his compatriot Yemmerrawanne to travel to England in 1792, he likely did so in the hope they might serve as mediators and possibly even negotiators for a future treaty. Since the seventeenth century, indigenous envoys from various nations had been sent to Britain by far-flung colonial officials to persuade those nations to establish formal alliances. The resultant treaties with Native Americans, Pacific Islanders and others were Britain's insurance policies should their enemies or competitors, such as France, threaten imperial expansion. Bennelong, who spent three years in England, was an expert politician who used marriages for himself and his sisters to forge allies with opposing factions, establishing and eventually extending his power within his Wangal clan.

Bennelong and Phillip's relationship stands as a leitmotif for Australian race relations: it started dramatically with a kidnapping (violence), then developed into an attempt to understand and negotiate, moved on to mutual misunderstandings and the exertion of power by the colonisers, and finished in silence. Bennelong walked away, Phillip retreated to England, and the opportunity was lost.

Australia's history is dotted with many similar stories, but our next place marker on the journey to the Voice took place over forty years later. As the colonial enterprise developed, a series of legal and regulatory regimes emerged. An early form of restrictive governance applied to Indigenous people originated in Melbourne. Uniquely in Australian terms, the settlement of Port Phillip in 1835 was accompanied by an attempted accord known as the (John) Batman Treaty. But the Sydney-based governor of New South Wales, Richard Burke, swiftly declared this document to be invalid, and the Colonial Office in London confirmed it as such. In short, the treaty was determined to be void as it was deemed impossible to establish a treaty with people who had no recognised polity—or political recognition.

It is also widely acknowledged that Victoria was the first Australian colony to develop and legislate a system of 'Aboriginal Protection'. Only fifteen years after Batman's arrival, there were already more than 75 000 settlers in the colony, most of whom had arrived in the previous decade. After the mid-nineteenth-century gold rush, this increased to just under 540 000, an enormous new population that rapidly displaced the Indigenous population. Even before the arrival of Batman, the European presence had been severely felt, with vast numbers of Kulin people ravaged by disease. Smallpox preceded Batman's party in two waves, with epidemics in the 1790s and 1820s. The disease tragically and drastically reduced the late-eighteenth-century Kulin population, which probably numbered at least 60 000 people, to somewhere between 10 000 and 15 000 people.[4]

Just a year or so after Batman and his group arrived, a different kind of power started to exert influence. In London, there was outrage at the damage caused by the settlers' invasion of the colony of Port Phillip. Much of this disquiet was motivated by the anti-slavery movement's concern for human rights. The House of Commons *Report from the Select Committee on Aborigines (British Settlements)* provided the most concrete evidence of the effort to contain the violence of colonisation throughout the empire. The 1837 document, greeted with disdain by settlers in various colonies, made forceful arguments for the humanitarian management of the impact of British settlement. The 'wild times' of Port Phillip were a common story. However, despite the Select Committee report and subsequent recommendations being prompted by humanitarian concerns and what those who held them regarded as good intentions, indigenous peoples were never consulted. The result was the imposition of paternalistic solutions that had the effect of subjugating rather than protecting.

Directly emerging from the House of Commons report, the colonial laws regarding Aboriginal peoples were cast as 'Protection Acts', usually with the stated aim of making arrangements for the safeguarding and management of Aboriginal people, such as in the *Aboriginal Protection Act 1869* (Vic.). But these laws actually permitted colonial governments to coerce and control all aspects of Aboriginal life, including allowing the removal of children from families for any reason, warehousing children in missions, and forcing others onto reserves. They effectively removed Indigenous people from their lands, and damaged the connection to culture for many. The colonial officials controlled who could marry, travel and work, and restricted their wages and autonomy. The Acts were assimilatory and functioned to break cultural practices, kinship relationships and personal autonomy, casting Aboriginal people as less than citizens, devoid of legal rights or identity—and in various forms, they persisted right into the late 1960s. All of which contributed to Stanner's cult of forgetfulness and the ensuing silence. For mainstream Australia, Indigenous Australia became a case of out of sight, out of mind.

Aboriginal people were never consulted about this, nor did they agree to being removed from their traditional lands. But they consistently asked to be heard. In the late nineteenth century, the recognised leader of the Wurundjeri people (of Melbourne) was William Barak, who was renowned for his advocacy work in asserting Aboriginal people's rights. As a child, Barak had been a witness to the signing of the short-lived Batman Treaty. On behalf of his community, Barak actively lobbied the government and authorities for land rights, land justice and improved treatment for Aboriginal people. He was instrumental in one of the nineteenth century's key claims made by Aboriginal people: the Coranderrk Petition. Coranderrk was a government-run Aboriginal reserve north of Melbourne where the Wurundjeri and other Aboriginal people had been confined. Despite assurances to the contrary, it became increasingly likely that the reserve would be reduced or eliminated, with the land being distributed to white farmers who lived nearby. In response, Barak and his neighbours gathered over 1800 signatures to petition the government to preserve the reserve.

The Coranderrk Petition was presented to the Victorian Government in 1886. It argued for the acknowledgement of Aboriginal land rights and the protection of Coranderrk as a permanent home for the Wurundjeri people. While the petition did not achieve all of its goals, it did raise awareness about the mistreatment of Aboriginal people and the need for land rights recognition. Ultimately, the Coranderrk Petition failed, but it stands as a case study of ongoing calls by Aboriginal people to be heard, to have a say in matters that affect them.[5]

These examples are drawn from Victoria, which was also home to the prominent Yorta Yorta political activist William Cooper. As a young man, Cooper witnessed his people successfully claim the reservation of land known as Cumeroogunga.[6] The Yorta Yorta managed the reserve, running a successful farming operation from the 1880s into the 1900s. Inevitably, in the 1920s, the Board for the Protection of Aborigines broke up communities and relocated families, and by the 1930s Cooper was serving as the secretary to the Australian Aborigines League, founded by the Melbourne Aboriginal community. Like Barak before him, Cooper circulated a petition calling for direct representation in parliament, enfranchisement and land rights. This was another poignant call to be heard.

In 1938, Cooper and other members of the Aborigines Progressive Association, which had been founded in Sydney the year before, led the first delegation to a prime minister to request federal oversight of Aboriginal concerns. By October 1937, he had gathered over 1800 petition signatures from Aboriginal people all over Australia. However, in March 1938, the Commonwealth chose not to forward the petition to King George VI, or to seek the constitutional amendment required to legislate for Aboriginal people or establish an Aboriginal constituency. This, from Cooper's perspective, was vital because Aboriginal people's ideas were not considered during the drafting of government laws affecting them.

There appears to be no surviving record of Cooper's petition, though many contemporary sources refer to it. The prime minister of the day, Joseph Lyons, never sent the petition to Buckingham Palace, so yet another opportunity to be heard was lost. However, as Bain Attwood describes in his biography of Cooper, Queen Elizabeth II eventually received another petition thanks to Cooper's grandson Boydie Turner's trip to London in 2014.

Petitioning was an often-used technique for making claims to the Commonwealth Government, an example of seeking to be heard, and we argue it has been foundational to contemporary requests for a Voice to Parliament. One group that has been particularly consistent and effective in their use of petitions is the Yolŋu of Arnhem Land. In 1963, the conservative federal government of Robert Menzies excised 300 square kilometres of land from the Arnhem Land (Aboriginal) Reserve and granted leases for bauxite mining. Elders were concerned about the effects this would have on the land and access to their sacred sites, not least because it was done without consulting them as traditional owners. The Yolŋu traditional owners created two bark petitions that documented their concerns and their request for a formal inquiry into the leases; one was in their own language, Yolŋu Matha, and the other was in English. The typed-out petitions were glued to bark sheets and included artwork from the Yolŋu moieties of Dhuwa and Yirritja. Visually powerful, they highlighted the Yolŋu people's assertion of their right to be heard, and to have a say in what happens on their land. As Marcia Langton and Aaron Corn show in their book *Law*, culture and law are intertwined, indistinguishable—you cannot have one without the other. The bark petitions were based on this relationship.[7]

The two petitions were partially successful in that the Yolŋu were heard, and the Select Committee on

Grievances of Yirrkala Aborigines, Arnhem Land Reserve, was established in parliament. Of course, despite this, the mining continued, but nonetheless the committee recognised the rights that the Yolŋu people had outlined and advised parliament to coordinate compensation, protect sacred sites, and form a mine-monitoring committee. The success of the 1963 petitions led to four more occasions when the Yolŋu used petitioning as a legal strategy.

In 1968, a petition was filed asking for the renaming of a nearby township to Nhulunbuy; the request was granted, and the town is still known by that name today. Twenty years later, a bark petition known as the Barunga Statement called for self-determination, land rights, Indigenous rights, and reparations. When the petition was handed to then prime minister Bob Hawke, he pledged to begin drafting a treaty by 1990. Hawke used the Yolŋu term *Makarrata*, which refers to a traditional dispute-resolution ceremony, to describe his approach. However, Hawke never fulfilled this commitment, and in regards to a treaty, the government yet again fell silent.

In 1998, another bark petition asked for the establishment of diplomatic conversations between Yolŋu leaders and the Australian Parliament.

Unfortunately, as the petition was handed directly to prime minister John Howard, rather than to the House of Representatives, as required, it was deemed void. The fourth bark treaty was similarly unsuccessful, handed directly to prime minister Kevin Rudd in 2008, immediately after he delivered an apology for child removals and the stolen generations.

It is not far-fetched to link the petitions of Yirrkala, William Cooper and William Barak as unstructured representations to government, informal attempts by Indigenous people to have a say in matters pertaining to their communities, nor that they were early proposals for a Voice to Parliament. At their core was a desire for constitutional change and recognition. In fact, the Voice to Parliament, the Uluru Statement from the Heart and the impending referendum should be seen as having a deep genealogy that extends back to the very first encounters between Australia's First Nations peoples and the colonising British. We argue, as many do, that now is the time to listen to and heed that long-called-for voice.

~

Until Federation in 1901, Australia was divided into six distinct colonies, each with its own government, set of laws and even military forces. They each issued their own stamps and collected customs, tariffs and taxes. The colonies even built their railway tracks using different gauges, which complicated the movement of goods and thereby trade in general. The new federal Constitution was meant to unite the colonies, but Indigenous people were left out of the national embrace, all but forgotten. Federation divided law-making power between the states and the new central parliament. In this division, Indigenous people were left to state management, and were only referred to in the negative, excluded from Commonwealth legislative power, not counted in the Census.

Many Indigenous and non-Indigenous Australians have since looked to 1967 as the high point of engagement with, and recognition of, Indigenous status, observing that surely the most substantial and resonant constitutional amendment occurred in that year's successful referendum. The poll itself was simple. Australian voters listened to Indigenous advocates who sought two key changes to the Constitution.

The first concerned the legislative power of the Australian Parliament in section 51(xxvi), which gave parliament limited power to make laws 'with respect to … the people of any race, other than the aboriginal race in any State, for whom it is deemed necessary to make special law'. To be clear, what this meant was that the federal parliament could make laws that conferred a special benefit, or imposed a special burden, on the people of one race—but not for, as they termed it, the 'aboriginal race'.

Indigenous Australians had been excluded from this provision for two fairly unpalatable reasons. The first was that the states wished to retain control over them. That might seem benign, but state legislation concerning Indigenous Australians was overwhelmingly discriminatory and caused great disadvantage. The second was that they were considered to be a dying race and not worthy of consideration.

As we mentioned earlier, state-based Protection Acts regularly dispossessed Indigenous people of their homes; broke up families, separating children from their parents; and instituted other discriminatory and assimilatory practices. The campaign to change section 51(xxvi) was strongly motivated by the belief that the federal parliament needed to be given power to make nationwide laws for Indigenous Australians, to redress this discrimination. So the Australian people were asked whether the words 'other than the aboriginal race in any State' should be removed from section 51(xxvi).

The second change concerned section 127 of the Constitution, which originally provided: 'In reckoning the numbers of the people of the Commonwealth … aboriginal natives shall not be counted'. The referendum asked whether section 127 should be removed so that Aboriginal people would be counted in the census.

The 1967 referendum was a watershed moment in Australian race relations and a pivotal moment in the country's legal history, as the proposed changes were approved by a majority of people, and a majority of states. In fact, 90.77 per cent of those who voted were in favour of the changes. It is unsurprising that these amendments passed as they had bipartisan support; there was no formal campaign to oppose them. However, in hindsight, it does not seem that the referendum achieved all that was hoped for. Despite the popular movement to address Indigenous disadvantage, there was no significant or immediate change. It appeared that the Australian nation had still not found a way to properly recognise, engage with and include Indigenous nations in the constitutional, legal and political functioning of the state. The fault line had not been repaired.

The first laws made under the new powers were not enacted until the Whitlam government.

Under the *Aboriginal and Torres Strait Islanders (Queensland Discriminatory Laws) Act 1975*, the federal government legislated to make discriminatory state laws inapplicable by overriding them, thereby attempting to eliminate racial discrimination against Indigenous Australians. It was on 16 August 1975 that Vincent Lingiari, a Gurindji Elder, received a handful of red dirt from prime minister Gough Whitlam. Whitlam had scooped up the soil after presenting to the Gurindji people the deeds of a small parcel of their traditional country, then known as Wave Hill Station. Whitlam remarked:

> Vincent Lingiari, I solemnly hand to you these deeds as proof, in Australian law, that these lands belong to the Gurindji people, and I put into your hands this piece of the earth itself as a sign that we restore them to you and your children forever.

But although this moment was evocative in terms of land rights, and provided a brilliantly iconic photo opportunity, it ultimately failed to advance political and legal relationships beyond the immediate Gurindji station. The Gurindji people had been heard, but their voice did not echo beyond them. Furthermore, the Gurindji did not get inalienable

Aboriginal freehold ownership deeds to the station until May 1986.

Despite the positives of the 1967 referendum outcome, it is important to note that the power granted can be used for *any* laws with respect to Aboriginal and Torres Strait Islander peoples. It does not stipulate that the laws need to be favourable; in fact, it enables detrimental laws to be passed as well. The aim of the referendum was to grant the federal government legislative power, but that power has not reliably been used to the advantage of the intended beneficiaries. Indigenous Australians are still disadvantaged, in many ways. Thus, the fault line endures. Both the benefit embedded in the *Native Title Act 1993* and the later detrimental treatment in the *Native Title Amendment Act 1998* demonstrate the capacity of legislative power to take away what was earlier granted.

These examples demonstrate the way in which Australian governments have continued to exercise power and develop policies *for* Aboriginal people, rarely *with* them, and almost never *by* them. The Voice to Parliament, as outlined in the Uluru Statement from the Heart, presents a once-in-a-lifetime opportunity to address this by foregrounding Indigenous views, front and centre.

LISTENING TO THE PRESENT

The fault line that meant Indigenous people were invisible in law, which as we have argued started with Cook and continued through the early decades of the federation, persisted until it was explicitly addressed in 1992, in *Mabo v Queensland (No 2)*. This ruling by the High Court of Australia rejected the legal fiction that the Australian territory had been unoccupied before 1788. And yet, the ruling only identified the fracture rather than fixing it, and consequently the enduring impacts and dire consequences of colonialism have not been remedied.

The landmark *Mabo* case needs to be set against a sole Australian legal authority, the single judgment of Justice Blackburn in *Milirrpum v Nabalco* (the *Gove Land Rights* case) in 1971. The Northern Territory Supreme Court had found that the laws of Australia could not sustain a claim for land title by the Yolŋu clans. This was because Justice Blackburn concluded that Australian common law had no capacity to recognise communal Aboriginal title, despite the self-evident existence and continued practising of law and customs by the people of Arnhem Land. Justice Blackburn found that Australia was different from New Zealand, Papua and New Guinea, Canada and all the other British territories. And what was that difference? Only that Cook and his successors had been unable to listen to and understand the claims of sovereignty and polity of the First Peoples on our shores.

In 1982, Eddie Koiki Mabo and his co-plaintiffs sought to be heard, bringing a claim for recognition of their ownership of lands on Murray Island in the far north of Torres Strait. One basis of their claim was that *Milirrpum v Nabalco* had been wrongly decided and had not formed a precedent. Australian law could, and must, recognise the Indigenous title of First Peoples.

After fighting its way through the courts for a decade, Mabo's claim was addressed in 1992 by the High Court, along with the fault line created by Cook's improper claim of possession of Australia. The court recognised that the unique property rights argued by the Torres Strait Islander claimants could be applied to recognition of their land rights 'as against the whole world'. And all Indigenous Australians could have their rights recognised. Justice Brennan wrote:

> Whatever the justification advanced in earlier days for refusing to recognize the rights and interests

> in land of the indigenous inhabitants of settled colonies, an unjust and discriminatory doctrine of that kind can no longer be accepted.[8]

The decision was significant because it opened the door for Aboriginal and Torres Strait Islander land claims beyond the existing land grants legislation; native title was a land title that came from the time before Cook and which could be recognised and enforced by contemporary First Nations, in certain constrained situations. The decision was also a landmark because it retained the central principles of the Australian land law, resource law and property law systems, and reaffirmed the constitutional basis for the establishment of the Australian nation, while allowing the recognition of native title rights and interests in lands and waters.

Of course, the decision also generated outrage and resistance from conservative representatives of the mining, pastoral and other rural industries. Mainstream media ran various stories implying that the ruling would spell the end of the Australian economy, that there would even be limitations on the use of domestic backyards, and that the 'guilt industry' and 'black armband' view of Australian history had gone too far.[9] With time, we can see that all the shock and outrage was misplaced. The law had simply changed, as it often does, and for some native title claimants, lands and waters were returned. Our national expectations of what was possible were expanded, albeit not greatly. And it was clear that our institutions, economy, politics and society could cope with such apparently significant shifts in institutional and legal arrangements.

The *Mabo* case put Indigenous issues firmly on the national agenda. Six months after the ruling, prime minister Paul Keating delivered an oration now known as the Redfern Statement. We do not think it an overstatement to suggest that this was another pivotal moment in Australian race relations. In a powerful, almost staccato-poetical delivery, Keating enunciated:

> It begins, I think, with that act of recognition.
> Recognition that it was we who did the dispossessing.
> We took the traditional lands and smashed the traditional way of life.
> We brought the diseases. The alcohol.
> We committed the murders.
> We took the children from their mothers.
> We practised discrimination and exclusion.
> It was our ignorance and our prejudice.

And our failure to imagine these things being done to us.

The following year, the Australian Parliament passed the *Native Title Act 1993*, and for a while at least, things looked very different. The preamble to the *Native Title Act* noted:

> The people whose descendants are now known as Aboriginal peoples and Torres Strait Islanders were the inhabitants of Australia before European settlement. They have been progressively dispossessed of their lands. This dispossession occurred largely without compensation, and successive governments have failed to reach a lasting and equitable agreement with Aboriginal peoples and Torres Strait Islanders concerning the use of their lands.

Each of the moments discussed—the 1967 referendum, the original *Mabo* decision and the *Native Title Act*—felt as if they had delivered a new paradigm, and new ways, to recognise the wrongs of the past, and the omissions and negligence of the present. These moments called on us to respond deeply, thoughtfully and actively to the calls for just relations with First Nations peoples. But while the movement grew, progress was slow. Keating grasped the opportunity that the *Mabo* case offered and seemed poised to make substantive changes that could have manifested in formal reconciliation and proper two-way dialogue. But although much touted, there has yet to be true reconciliation.

~

Two key reports similarly punctuate the journey from the cult of forgetfulness and silence to contemporary calls for recognition and justice, and the request to be heard on all relevant matters, so forming part of the foundational narrative that ends with a Voice to Parliament. While there have been many thoughtful and respected inquiries, commissions and reports on issues of Indigenous disadvantage, the *Final Report of the Royal Commission into Aboriginal Deaths in Custody* (1991) and the *Bringing Them Home Report* (1997) serve as landmark moments, challenging the silence over the impact that Australian laws and policies have had on Indigenous peoples.

In 1987, after a public outcry at the death in custody of sixteen-year-old John Pat at the hands of police officers in Roebourne, Western Australia four years earlier, a royal commission was established to investigate the causes of deaths of Aboriginal people in the nation's prisons. This was known as the Royal Commission into Aboriginal Deaths in Custody (RCIADIC). A federal judge, James Muirhead QC, was initially appointed chair of the commission on his own, but with an ever-widening number of deaths under investigation, a further five commissioners were included, including Yawuru Elder (and now senator) Patrick Dodson, the only Indigenous commissioner. With the expansion of the number of commissioners also came an expansion of the terms of reference: the commission was tasked with looking beyond the specific circumstances of individual deaths to the broader social conditions that contributed to the presence of people in custody, as well as the nature and causes of over-incarceration of Indigenous people.

The final RCIADIC report was devastating in two senses. First, it catalogued and spotlit ninety-nine unnecessarily brutal and painful deaths in custody. Second, the report offered an indictment of Australian criminal justice systems that embedded discriminatory processes and policies targeting Aboriginal and Torres Strait Islander peoples for disproportionate policing, incarceration and neglect. The vast majority of the cases examined by the royal commission involved people who suffered dislocation, dispossession, and removal from family and culture. This brought to the forefront the relationship between child removals and cultural damage, and over-engagement with the criminal justice systems. In fact, Aboriginal children removed from their families often immediately became wards of the state and simultaneously gained a criminal record, thus sparking a lifetime of adverse treatment.

In 1995, the Human Rights and Equal Opportunity Commission (HREOC; now the Australian Human Rights Commission) commenced a 'National Enquiry into the Separation of Aboriginal and Torres Strait Islander Children from Their Families'. This was a comprehensive investigation into child removals and the emergence of what became popularly known as the stolen generations. In 1997 HREOC delivered the report *Bringing Them Home*, according to which Indigenous children were systematically taken from their families between 1910 and 1970 and either placed in institutions or adopted by non-Indigenous families. It made the case that these removals constituted a gross violation of human rights and emphasised the terrible consequences of these government actions on Indigenous families and communities. In the two-and-a-half decades since its release, the report has, in many ways, given decision-makers and the legal system a framework for considering these consequences. In 2008, for example, the Australian Parliament apologised to Indigenous people for the pain previous generations had endured.

Tragically, however, not much has changed on both fronts. Most disturbingly, there are still too many Indigenous people behind bars, and far too many of them die there. This lack of progress was arguably flagged by a series of backward steps in the late 1990s and early 2000s. These regressions included John Howard's amendments to the *Native Title Act* in 1998 and the demolition six years later of the Aboriginal and Torres Strait Islander Commission (ATSIC), which tipped the balance away from First Nations people's rights. The next low point was the Northern Territory Intervention, when dramatic and coercive mechanisms were put in place in a wide range of Aboriginal communities, on spurious justification and without consultation.

The Howard Liberal–National Coalition government enacted the *Northern Territory National Emergency Response Act*, or 'the Intervention', in August 2007. Liberal politicians framed the Intervention as an immediate response and solution to problems within Indigenous communities in the Northern Territory, including issues relating to health, housing, employment and justice. Some were highlighted in the report of the Board of Inquiry into the Protection of Aboriginal Children from Sexual Abuse, titled *Ampe Akelyernemane Meke Mekarle: 'Little Children Are Sacred'*, and prepared by Rex Wild QC and Alyawarre Elder and social justice advocate (now a key proponent of the Uluru Statement) Pat Anderson. However, the first and primary recommendation of *Little Children Are Sacred* was that governments commit to meaningful consultation with Aboriginal people when implementing Aboriginal community initiatives. Yet another instance of a request to be listened to that largely has been overlooked.

The Intervention was rushed into place just a few weeks after *Little Children Are Sacred* was handed down, with debate over the *Emergency Response Act* abbreviated and breathless in its speedy passage through the federal parliament. It was the antithesis of self-determination.[10] Even subsequent changes of government merely saw the Intervention reframed, such as when the Kevin Rudd government focused the policy on 'Closing the Gap' in 2008.

Closing the Gap is a shorthand statement that refers to the significant differences in health outcomes and life expectancy between Aboriginal and Torres Strait Islander peoples and non-Indigenous Australians.[11] This gap will hopefully be closed within one generation. Closing the Gap is based on the premise that Aboriginal and Torres Strait Islander peoples have better life outcomes when they are involved in policy, program and service creation, as demonstrated by the success of the National Aboriginal Controlled Health Organisations. It also recognises that structural change in how governments engage with Aboriginal and Torres Strait Islander peoples is necessary for success. The Voice to Parliament will have a role to play here—Fiona Stanley and Marcia Langton address this in 'How the Voice Can Help Close the Gap', highlighting the pragmatic steps that can be taken.[12]

~

We can see that, on many occasions throughout our nation's history, change seemed imminent, perhaps even just on the horizon, but it always receded into the distance. The instigation and then closure of successive important representative organisations such as the National Aboriginal Consultative Committee, the National Aboriginal Conference, the Aboriginal and Torres Strait Islander Commission, and the National

Congress of Australia's First Peoples illustrates the impacts of electoral politics and the vagaries of political ideologies. Each decade seems to have brought a different structure, some more and some less representative than others. But there has been little continuity or coherence, in either the national or state administrative and political arrangements, in addressing the specific concerns of Indigenous people.

In stark contrast, the 2017 Uluru Statement from the Heart deliberately asserts the authority of Aboriginal and Torres Strait Islander Australians over the key claims for sovereignty and self-determination—well-known and accepted concepts of political autonomy and authority in international law. The statement declares these concepts are based on spiritual connection to, and being first possessors of, the land of Australia. The statement's claim to authority represents a pluralist expression of law, a concept that is common in countries that are former colonies where a traditional (or customary) legal system sits alongside the laws of the former colonial authority. Australia can accommodate many laws, many people and many nations.

The Uluru Statement calls for two substantive reforms. The first is constitutional amendment to incorporate a 'Voice to Parliament', an advisory body of Indigenous representatives that would influence and participate in the development of Commonwealth law and policy regarding matters that impact Indigenous communities and peoples. Constitutional entrenchment, rather than simple legislative enactment, is sought to protect the advisory body against dissolution due to changes in political support for such a body, and also to engender popular support for the recognition of Aboriginal and Torres Strait peoples' rights in the Constitution.

The second reform is the establishment of a Makarrata Commission, an agreement-making body with responsibilities for developing treaty, or agreement-making processes, and supporting a national truth-telling process about history, past abuses and colonisation, among other matters.

Together, these reforms are expressed in the Uluru Statement as 'Voice, Treaty, Truth'. We understand these elements as working in concert to deliver structural and substantive reform to the legal and political processes that have until now excluded Indigenous sovereignty and self-determination from Anglo-Australian public law.

The referendum process itself may have wider effects on Australian society at large, much as the 1967 referendum and the national apology each represented a nationwide shift in attitudes. Given that Australian public law and public policy have generally been dismissive, derogatory and often destructive towards Indigenous laws and governance structures, there are strong arguments for the federal Constitution to include acknowledgment of the first occupation, ownership and sovereignty of Australia by Indigenous peoples.

Now, through the broad Indigenous community consultations that led to the Uluru Statement from the Heart, through numerous Australian parliamentary committees and inquiries, through the affirmation of governments, many law-makers, civil society organisations and the private sector, we have a proposal for an Indigenous-led advisory body known as the 'Aboriginal and Torres Strait Islander Voice'. That advisory body would be included in our Australian Constitution by way of the upcoming referendum, which is the only way we can alter the words of our constitutional document. And it needs to be in the Constitution, not only to protect the body from the changing whims of governments, but also because this is what the Uluru Statement asks of us:

> With substantive constitutional change and structural reform, we believe this ancient sovereignty can

> shine through as a fuller expression of Australia's nationhood … We seek constitutional reforms to empower our people and take a rightful place in our own country.

Despite the political debate that has ensued around the Voice proposal, we observe that the choice of an institutional advisory body that informs parliament and the executive government is entirely unremarkable. It is a modest proposal. We barely cast a glance at the work of the Productivity Commission or the Australian Law Reform Commission (ALRC), both of which are mainstream advisory bodies to the national government. They *inform* law-making; their advice may be considered, or not. Similarly, the Voice to Parliament will have the capacity to inform policy and reform, but it is not a third chamber of parliament. It will not make laws or distribute funding. It will not undertake program delivery. It will have no veto. The Bill that amends the Constitution makes it clear that 'The Parliament shall have power to make laws with respect to matters relating to the Aboriginal and Torres Strait Islander Voice, including its composition, functions, powers and procedures'. Parliament retains control over the way the Voice works.

There are already a series of guiding principles as to what the Voice will be, how it will be composed and how it will operate. The Calma and Langton report titled *Indigenous Voice Co-design Process: Final Report to the Australian Government*, delivered in late 2021, sets out some key frameworks for how the Voice would work. Like any government agency or advisory body, the final structure and arrangements for the Voice will be decided by parliament when it passes the laws that establish the body. So politicians will retain the final say on how the Voice operates, while the existence of the body is enshrined in the Constitution.

The Calma and Langton co-design report was based on widespread consultation and feedback within communities. The model they propose would have twenty-four representative members, comprising state and territory representatives, Torres Strait representatives, and five additional representatives from remote areas around Australia. It would be gender-balanced and include youth representatives. The members would be selected by Aboriginal and Torres Strait Islander communities, not appointed by the executive government, and they would serve on the Voice for a fixed period to ensure regular accountability to their communities. Also with respect to accountability, as well as transparency, it is intended that the Voice be subject to standard governance and reporting requirements, and its members would come within the scope of the newly established federal National Anti-Corruption Commission.

Once established, the Voice would be tasked with making representations to parliament and the executive government on matters relating to Aboriginal and Torres Strait Islander peoples. The Voice would be funded to adequately research, develop and make these representations, which could be in response to requests from the government and parliament (just as the ALRC responds to references from the government), or they could be proactive representations (just as the Victorian Law Reform Commission is able to initiate its own inquiries). And of course, ideally, the parliament and executive government would seek representations from the Voice early in the development of proposed laws and policies.

If the referendum is successful, a process will be undertaken, involving Aboriginal and Torres Strait Islander communities, the parliament and the broader public, to definitively settle the design of the Voice. The legislation to establish the Voice will then proceed through standard parliamentary processes to ensure adequate scrutiny by elected representatives in both houses of parliament. Only then will membership of the Voice be decided, and the process of feeding advisory representations to parliament and the government begin.

There are many other valid bases for addressing the potential impact of the Voice, be they moral, ethical, philosophical, economic, policy or political rationales, but next we will canvas the national values and goals that flow from having the Voice structured in this way, and having this advisory role. In this sense, we engage here with the question of the national interest of the Voice body.

The Voice provides constitutional recognition

The proposed Voice achieves constitutional recognition according to the priorities of First Nations peoples. This recognition is in alignment with a series of constitutional decisions, notably in *Mabo* (1992) and most recently in *Love, Thoms v. Commonwealth* (2020). In these cases, the High Court affirmed the unique constitutional status of the First Nations peoples of Australia by reason of their ancient and continuing connection to the nation's lands and waters. The form of the Voice referendum proposal is the culmination of a considerable body of independent work on constitutional recognition, including that of the Referendum Council, the Uluru Dialogues, and the Voice Co-design Process. This work brought together First Nations peoples and non-Indigenous experts and expresses the consensus position of First Nations peoples as to the form and goals of constitutional recognition. The specific form, membership and design of the Voice body itself will come later, although the design principles have already been mapped out.

The Voice, and the referendum to amend the Constitution, also address our Constitution's silence by acknowledging Aboriginal and Torres Strait Islander peoples as the First Peoples of this land. But this is more than merely symbolic recognition. It gives substantive recognition by creating and entrenching an advisory body that directly addresses the systemic barriers facing First Nations peoples. It brings the experience of First Nations peoples into Australian governance structures by empowering Indigenous people to make representations to parliament and the agencies of the government. Just as we see with other representative institutions, such as law reform commissions, advisory commissions, royal commissions and parliamentary inquiries, the Voice can enhance good governance by entrenching institutional processes informed by modern best practices and community representation.

The Voice upholds parliamentary supremacy and the efficient functioning of the executive

Importantly for the integrity of Australia's system of government, the Voice operates within the institutional framework of the nation. The threats and fears of what it might do, or what powers it might have, are misplaced.

As a matter of law and statutory and constitutional interpretation, the proposal presents no challenge or threat to Australia's territorial integrity or established norms of governance. The power of the Voice is to make representations: it is merely a permanent advisory body. This advisory status has been made evident in the plain language of the Constitution Alteration (Aboriginal and Torres Strait Islander Voice) 2023 Bill and the supporting explanatory memorandum. The second reading speech describes the proposal as 'a form of constitutional recognition that is practical and substantive' and is called for by First Nations peoples in the Uluru Statement. The proposal does not have any of the powers of a house of parliament, such as the ability to make laws or appropriate funds.

The Voice is constitutionally conservative as it maintains parliamentary supremacy and the proper functioning of the executive government.

The capacity to make representations to the executive government at the early stages of the development of a bill or policy, and suggesting legislative or policy reform, works to enhance governance. Representations to the government permit the opportunity to consider relevant data, information and advice, to improve a policy or law before parliament passes legislation. In addition, much of what is relevant to Aboriginal and Torres Strait Islander peoples occurs through policy and its administration, funding and implementation—there is more than just the law at stake. Representations from the Voice to government provide the opportunity for improvement of service delivery and outcomes according to the identified needs of the relevant communities.

The Voice fulfils the requirements of international human rights law

International law anticipates and expresses the need for self-determination, and it already recognises that indigenous peoples have particular rights.

Professor James Anaya, the former special rapporteur on the rights of indigenous peoples and a legal expert, defines indigenous peoples as the 'living descendants of pre-invasion inhabitants of lands now dominated by others. They are culturally distinct groups that find themselves engulfed by other settler societies born of forces of empire and conquest.'[13]

Human rights law embraces the right to self-determination and the right to free, prior and informed consent as fundamental to indigenous peoples, as recognised in the UN Declaration on the Rights of Indigenous Peoples (UNDRIP).[14] In 2009, Australia formally endorsed UNDRIP, which, as a declaration of the UN General Assembly, forms part of the body of international law to which Australia is a party, and to which we have obligations. The rights that UNDRIP affirms are grounded in binding international treaties, such as the International Covenant on Civil and Political Rights (ICCPR) and the International Covenant on Economic, Social and Cultural Rights. Australia has both signed and ratified these covenants, which have a common Article 1 regarding self-determination:

> All peoples have a right to self-determination. By virtue of that right they freely determine their

> political status and freely pursue their economic, social and cultural development.

Self-determination should be understood as a constructive, inclusive concept, rather than as a threat to the state. Anaya explains the ways in which indigenous self-determination can manifest as both 'constitutive' and as continuing or 'ongoing'. He proposes that 'constitutive' self-determination requires the governing institutional order be created by processes that are 'guided by the will of the peoples who are governed', that the political order should reflect 'the collective will of the peoples concerned', and that to meet that standard, there must be the participation and consent of the governed peoples, particularly in times of institutional development and reform.

Anaya also noted that self-determination has an ongoing component. It needs the establishment and maintenance of institutions 'under which individuals and groups are able to make meaningful choices in matters touching upon all spheres of life on a continuous basis'.[15] In Australia, this means there is an obligation to develop institutional frameworks that include First Nations peoples in the decisions, processes, law-making and administration that impact their lives.

The Voice reinstates self-determination

The Voice reinstates self-determination in three key ways. First, having the Constitution state that Aboriginal and Torres Strait Islander peoples are the First Peoples of Australia recognises their unique and special status as Indigenous people within the fabric of Australia's constitutional framework.

Second, the Voice manifests the self-determination of First Nations peoples, providing an institutional mechanism through which they can exercise autonomy in matters relating to Indigenous affairs and 'participate in decision-making in matters which would affect their rights' through representatives they have chosen for their own Indigenous decision-making institutions.[16] Through this advisory body, the polity can engage in good faith with First Nations peoples 'to obtain their free, prior, and informed consent before adopting and implementing legislative or administrative measures that may affect them'.[17]

Finally, the various processes and consultations leading to the proposal, particularly the Uluru Dialogues and the Uluru Statement, are themselves exercises of self-determination by First Nations peoples. The Voice proposal has not been generated by the government but has resulted from the express invitation of First Nations peoples themselves through the Uluru Statement.

Other human rights standards and treaties are also applicable to this obligation to guarantee participation and consent, such as the ICCPR's Article 25, which guarantees rights of political participation, as well as its Article 27 on the protection of minority rights and articles 2, 3 and 26, which guarantee non-discrimination. There is not the scope here to fully analyse the Voice through the human rights law framework, but we do observe that the inclusion of the Voice within Australia's political and legal structures brings us into closer alignment with the international human rights obligations that have been accepted but are yet to be fully implemented.

~

In addition to the application of international law and human rights standards, we should also look to Australia's common-law cousins. Key nations that inherited a similar legal legacy through the process of British colonial expansion in the eighteenth century developed legal and constitutional mechanisms for establishing proper lawful relations with their indigenous communities, whether as domestic dependent nations, tribes or citizens. These mechanisms, albeit dishonoured and undermined for decades, are regarded as largely supportive of indigenous rights and legal recognition. The Canadian modern treaty processes and the New Zealand Waitangi Tribunal settlement processes, for example, show us how anglophone common-law polities can adjust to the incorporation and resolution of indigenous claims and become pluralistic polities. In the United States, the significance of the legal relations that the Creek and Cherokee nations have with the state of Oklahoma goes beyond the resolution of jurisdiction for tax purposes, just as the Waitangi processes speak to more than land claims alone. The very fact of modern, formal, legal engagement between peoples gives rise to a different culture of responsibility, respect and recognition.

By way of contrast, consider Canada, a federal nation with very similar British legal and political antecedents to Australia's. Canadian Aboriginal rights are recognised as inherent rights held by indigenous peoples in Canada based on their historical occupancy and use of the land. Section 35 of the Canadian *Constitution Act, 1982* recognises and protects 'the existing aboriginal and treaty rights of the aboriginal peoples of Canada'. In Canada the term 'Aboriginal' includes First Nations, Inuit and Métis peoples, each of whom have distinct rights and cultural identities. While section 35 recognises Aboriginal rights, it did not create those rights; they existed before the Canadian *Constitution Act*. It also does not define those rights but instead leaves this work to the country's highest court, the Supreme Court. So, in Canada, Aboriginal rights are understood to include a collection of cultural, social, political and economic rights, including rights to land, as well as to fish, hunt, practise culture and establish treaties. They also include rights to self-government, language and traditional practices.

Canada's Supreme Court has played a significant role in shaping the understanding and interpretation of Aboriginal rights through a series of landmark decisions, such as the Sparrow, Calder, Delgamuukw and Tsilhqot'in cases. These cases have affirmed that Aboriginal rights are not extinguished and must be upheld and accommodated by the Canadian Government. Despite this progress, serious challenges remain. Issues such as land and resource disputes, socioeconomic inequalities and the implementation of self-government agreements continue to prompt contested debates. However, it does seem that the national discourse on reconciliation and full implementation of Aboriginal rights embraces ongoing dialogue, partnership and collaboration between indigenous peoples, the government and wider Canadian society. In Canada, constitutional recognition was not a singular event but rather remains an ongoing process. In this sense, constitutional recognition of, and respect for, Aboriginal rights is treated not only as a legal obligation but also as a fundamental part of the national journey towards greater justice, equality and healing for indigenous communities in Canada.

New Zealand, while having the same British legal antecedents as Canada and Australia, differs again. It is a unicameral and unitary state, not a federal one, and its constitution is not found in a single document. That said, the *Constitution Act 1986* is a key formal statement of New Zealand's system of government, and, increasingly, the country's constitution reflects the Treaty of Waitangi as a founding document. Thus, Māori constitutional rights are grounded in this historic treaty, signed in 1840 between the British Crown and Māori chiefs. The treaty is now considered the foundation of the relationship between the government and Māori, recognising and guaranteeing the rights, interests and protection of

Māori culture, lands and resources, and so ensuring their cultural and economic wellbeing. The Treaty of Waitangi also establishes principles of partnership and participation, affirming Māori as equal partners in the governance of New Zealand and recognising their right to self-determination.

The interpretation of Māori constitutional rights has evolved through court decisions, legislation and treaty settlements. The Waitangi Tribunal, established in 1975, has played a significant national role in addressing historical injustices and ensuring the government's compliance with treaty principles. Māori constitutional rights now encompass language and cultural recovery, participation in decision-making processes, representation in government institutions including parliament, and resource management. The recognition of these rights aims to redress past injustices, promote contemporary social cohesion, and support Māori aspirations for self-governance and cultural continuity.

While Māori constitutional rights have advanced over the last fifty years, challenges do persist, particularly in areas such as land ownership, socioeconomic disparities and the full implementation of treaty settlements. As in Canada, ongoing dialogue, consultation and collaboration between the government and indigenous communities is considered crucial to meaningful and effective protection of Māori rights in New Zealand.

And so, in both Canada and New Zealand, we observe that constitutional recognition, along with meaningful dialogue and political participation, informs the operation of government. Structural and institutional mechanisms ensure these First Nations have a voice and that they are heard.

~

Despite the myriad positive consequences of the Voice as described above, many myths and much misinformation has been propagated about it. Certain concerns that have arisen at the time of writing will no doubt have dissipated with greater understanding of the proposal, while a number of counter-claims regarding the Voice have no foundation, as countless constitutional experts have testified.

To be clear, what is proposed is a Voice *to* Parliament, not a Voice *in* Parliament. It will have no role in passing legislation; that will remain in the hands of elected representatives in the federal parliament, as required by the Constitution. The Voice can make representations to parliament, but it will be up to parliament to decide what it does with those representations; it should pay attention to them, but it will always take into account a wide range of advice from across the community. The Voice does not create special rights for Indigenous people or give them a veto—it just establishes an advisory body. Parliament will be better informed about the impact of proposed laws on First Nations peoples and can amend its laws where that is appropriate. So, for example, it will inform how Closing the Gap and other initiatives can best work to improve outcomes.

The Voice will not damage our democratic institutions; it will enhance them. It will not 'put race into the Constitution', as the Constitution already allows for racially discriminatory laws by virtue of section 51(xxvi) (the race power). It will ensure that the silence and omissions of the past can be addressed in the future. It cannot be racist to address racism.

LISTENING TO THE VOICES

There is generosity in the Uluru Statement from the Heart. It is an invitation to commence a journey, Indigenous and non-Indigenous together, our nation as one. It is true reconciliation. The statement asserts:

With substantive constitutional change and structural reform, we believe this ancient sovereignty can shine through as a fuller expression of Australia's nationhood.

Proportionally, we are the most incarcerated people on the planet. We are not an innately criminal people. Our children are aliened from their families at unprecedented rates. This cannot be because we have no love for them. And our youth languish in detention in obscene numbers. They should be our hope for the future.

These dimensions of our crisis tell plainly the structural nature of our problem. This is the torment of our powerlessness.

We seek constitutional reforms to empower our people and take a rightful place in our own country. When we have power over our destiny our children will flourish. They will walk in two worlds and their culture will be a gift to their country.

In order to properly engage with the invitation posed in the Uluru Statement from the Heart, we have listened to the words of colleagues, Elders and experts, those who have worked on the proposal for a representative body that conforms with the call from the Uluru Dialogues as well as calls from throughout Australia's history.

The benefits of the Voice to Parliament are manifold. The proposal seeks to provide a platform for Indigenous people to directly influence government decision-making processes, fostering self-determination and advancing reconciliation. It is designed to enhance democratic functioning in Australia. Australia's Indigenous people have endured centuries of marginalisation, dispossession and systemic discrimination, but recognition of their inherent status, rights and needs has necessarily gained traction over the years. An Indigenous Voice to Parliament would offer a tangible step towards addressing the historical injustices suffered by Indigenous communities and forging better policies and laws to help resolve immediate issues.

Central to the design of the Voice is the principle of genuine self-determination. By granting Indigenous people a formal role in decision-making processes, this initiative empowers Indigenous communities to shape policies, programs and legislation that addresses their unique needs, aspirations and concerns. And from a national perspective, the inclusion of Indigenous voices will ensure that laws and initiatives are developed via a fundamental engagement with, and understanding of, Indigenous cultures, contexts, perspectives and priorities. This will immediately mitigate the risk of implementing ineffective or inappropriate measures that fail to adequately address the complexities of Indigenous issues. The enhanced policy relevance will result in more effective outcomes, improving the socioeconomic conditions and overall wellbeing of Indigenous communities.

By recognising the diversity and plurality of Australia's peoples and polities, the Voice also contributes to the building of a stronger, more inclusive nation. Indigenous representation will bridge the gap between the political system and the aspirations of Indigenous people, promoting social cohesion and unity. To have proper reconciliation between Indigenous and non-Indigenous Australians, we do need institutional structures that embed meaningful engagement, acknowledgment of past injustices, and concerted efforts towards structural change. This is what is meant by the refrain of 'Voice, Treaty, Truth'. The Voice will facilitate ongoing dialogue, promote mutual understanding, and foster trust between Indigenous communities and broader Australian society.

Indigenous cultures, kinship and languages hold significant value and are vital to Australia's cultural identity. By ensuring Indigenous representation, cultural heritage can be better protected, and Indigenous knowledge systems can become part of the fabric of governance and policymaking. And by recognising the unique historical and contemporary challenges faced by Indigenous communities, Australia can take the next steps in building a more equitable society, fostering a stronger nation that values and respects the rights and contributions of all its citizens.

~

We set out here some important voices that explain why they have advocated for the current proposal. But first, let us revisit some of the work that led up to it.

A series of discussions held in 2014–15 by Indigenous and non-Indigenous experts closely examined the proposals for constitutional recognition, the options for a non-discrimination clause, a preamble, and other approaches. This foundational work by some of Australia's foremost legal minds—Megan Davis, Gabrielle Appleby, Noel Pearson, Shireen Morris, George Williams, Anne Twomey, Greg Craven and others—settled on a dialogue model rather than a mere recognition model.[18] Then, in 2016–17, the Referendum Council undertook a series of thirteen First Nations Constitutional Dialogues to talk about constitutional change possibilities and to make sure that Aboriginal decision-making was at the centre of the reform process. To confirm the outcomes of these regional dialogues, in May 2017 the Referendum Council convened the National First Nations Constitutional Convention at Uluru. The delegates generously offered the Australian people the Uluru Statement from the Heart, and it received an overwhelmingly positive response. The Referendum Council's final report was delivered to then prime minister Malcolm Turnbull.[19] However, perhaps for overtly political reasons, such as the need to appease critics in Turnbull's own government, his administration hastily rejected the Voice to Parliament request.

In 2018, a joint select committee of parliament was convened to consider the work of the Referendum Council, chaired by Australian Labor Party Senator Patrick Dodson and Liberal Senator Julian Leeser.[20] In its final report, the committee found the Voice was the only viable Indigenous recognition proposal and recommended that the government 'initiate a process of co-design [of the Voice] with Aboriginal and Torres Strait Islander peoples'. The co-design process commenced the following year. In May 2022, new Prime Minister Anthony Albanese noted in his election victory speech that he was committed to implementing the Uluru Statement in full.

Tom Calma and Marcia Langton described the importance of the Voice in the foreword to the *Indigenous Voice Co-design Process: Final Report to the Australian Government*, which is worth quoting at length:

> We propose a strong, resilient and flexible system in which Aboriginal and Torres Strait Islander peoples and our communities will be part of genuine shared decision-making with governments at the local and regional level and have our voices heard by the Australian Parliament and Government in policy and law making. A voice to the Australian Parliament and Government would complement and amplify existing structures, and would not replace the role for these structures to continue to work with Government within their mandates. An Indigenous Voice will provide the right mechanism, working with and strengthening existing arrangements, for the voices of Aboriginal and Torres Strait Islander peoples to be heard on issues that affect us. The consideration of our vast

> experiences and diverse perspectives will lead to better policy outcomes, strengthen legislation and programs and, importantly, achieve better outcomes for our people.[21]

Lest anyone think that this tome was not both comprehensive and detailed, the Calma and Langton report was based on interviews with 9478 people and organisations, 115 community consultations in sixty-seven separate locations, 2978 submissions, 1127 surveys, 124 stakeholder meetings, and thirteen webinars. Unfortunately, few people have properly acquainted themselves with this document, which contains over 260 pages of carefully reasoned, well-supported arguments clearly articulating the necessity of a Voice to Parliament. As Professor Langton has pointed out on more than one occasion in the media, to understand what is being proposed, people need to be prepared to read the report. Much of the misinformation currently being touted could then be easily dismissed. The 'No' campaign's trite slogan 'If you don't know, vote no' is a case in point. Surely, rather than spreading ignorance, it might be better to suggest that if you don't know, then find out! Reading the Calma and Langton report would be a good place to start.

A 'No' vote is *not* a vote for the status quo. It will not have the effect of keeping the arrangements for managing Indigenous affairs as they are now. Rather, a negative result in the referendum will mean a loss of credibility, at a number of levels. It will amount to the end of reconciliation advocacy for many Indigenous leaders and their supporters. As Palawa scholar Ian Anderson put it in an opinion piece, a failed referendum will 'spell the end of the long reconciliation walk'.[22]

Anderson's view is shared by many who have focused their efforts on developing coherent and constructive advocacy for Indigenous recognition. Noel Pearson says he will 'fall silent' if the referendum fails, adding:

> If the advocacy of that pathway fails, well, then … a whole generation of Indigenous leadership will have failed because we will have advocated coming together in partnership with government and we would have made an invitation to the Australian people that was repudiated.[23]

But a loss will reverberate in other ways. Professor Marcia Langton states it clearly in the title of a recent article: 'If yes campaign for Indigenous voice loses "racists will feel emboldened".'[24] We have already watched aghast as leading Indigenous journalist and media identity Stan Grant stepped away from his national role on the ABC's flagship *Q+A* program, pointing out the impact of corrosive racist discourse. We have already seen some mainstream and social media debate about the Voice referendum become divisive and hostile to Indigenous people, with abusive racism deployed to attack the proposal. An unsuccessful referendum will mean that, instead of moving towards a more united, mature and thoughtful nation, we will see greater division and disrespect.

There is, unsurprisingly, disagreement about the proposal across Indigenous communities, although opinion polls suggest most Indigenous community members support the Voice. Among the very few exceptions are businessman and entrepreneur Nyunggai Warren Mundine and Country Liberal Senator Jacinta Nampijinpa Price. It is important that we respect differences of opinion and recognise that there has never been one unified Indigenous point of view. As we would expect when discussing hundreds of different cultures, there will always be divergences along with alignments.

Another critic is the independent Senator Lidia Thorpe, who argues that as it stands, the Voice does not go far enough. She is concerned that it does not include an acknowledgement of sovereignty: 'Sovereignty Never Ceded'. Ian Anderson notes that 'most Indigenous Australians who don't support the Voice do so because they think its ambitions are too modest. They do not think governments can or should be trusted.'[25] Indeed, past experiences such as the Howard government's abolition of ATSIC and the Hawke government's failed Makarrata process suggest that, by and large, governments can't be fully trusted. This is why proponents of the Voice are clear that they will need to be ever vigilant. This is the very reason the Uluru Statement calls for constitutional recognition and permanency, not merely an Act of parliament.

To those who seek more than the Voice, believing it falls short because it does not put in place treaty arrangements or a truth-telling commission, we say we agree. It is a modest first step. But if this step falters, the other steps will not occur. There will be little political or electoral will to pursue the agenda set out in the Uluru Statement, and all aspirations for justice and proper legal relations with First Nations peoples will be delayed indefinitely.

The effects of a failed referendum would not only be felt in Australia. It would amount to an international humiliation. This is a point powerfully made by Michelle Grattan in an opinion piece for *The Conversation*.[26] International scrutiny is upon us, and our international credibility matters—not just in terms of trade, education and employment, but also for our strategic standing as a middle power, and our leadership in our region. We are the only First World nation with Indigenous people and a colonial history that fails to recognise its First Nations peoples in its constitution.[27] Besides which, we have agreed to international treaties and declarations that recognise self-determination, so in regards to international law, we are obligated to protect and promote the recognition of Indigenous people's rights and status. If we cannot successfully mobilise a national consensus to respond meaningfully to the Uluru Statement and give a voice to Indigenous Australians, we will remain a diminished, weakened nation.

In an attempt to counter this important point, conservative commentators often remark that Indigenous Australians, comprising as they do less than 4 per cent of the population, should not receive special recognition, rights or representation. We firmly believe that this is a mischievous attempt to obscure the special status of being and belonging to our First Nations. As mentioned earlier, the

High Court has already recognised this special status. It is part of our constitutional law. It now needs to be part of our Constitution.

One of the most public faces of the Voice debate has been Wamba Wamba First Nations public lawyer Eddie Synot. Synot has been diligent on social media, constantly correcting misinformation and deliberate obfuscation. During an Australian Institute of Administrative Law conference at the University of New South Wales in October 2021, he noted how a First Nations Voice to Parliament would make a difference to the culture of power and decision-making with respect to Indigenous peoples. Synot drew on Juukan Gorge, where multinational mining company Rio Tinto destroyed a 46 000-year-old Aboriginal sacred site, as an example, arguing that the establishment of a Voice to Parliament would prevent a repeat of this situation. He said it was necessary to ensure that the rules are fair and transparent, that Indigenous voices are heard and respected, and that decision-making isn't just process-oriented but actively engaged in building a better future for all Australians. As Synot noted, 'It's not just a matter of changing the game's rules. It's [about] changing the game.'[28]

As we mentioned earlier, Noel Pearson is one of the significant legal minds behind this quest for recognition and reconciliation. Over the past thirty years, Pearson has maintained a national presence as he has advocated and agitated for Indigenous rights. As an activist, political leader and, importantly, a lawyer, he was an early proponent of constitutional recognition, and he recently observed that if the vote is unsuccessful, reconciliation efforts would be 'dead' and he could foresee years of unrest. A yes vote, on the other hand, would result in 'tectonic' improvements for the country. As he emphasised in an article, 'The country is going to change the minute we vote on this, and change for the better. We'll put a lot of bad things behind us when we do this. It's a simple change, but it's very profound.'[29]

Rachel Perkins, filmmaker and Indigenous advocate, and daughter of the legendary Aboriginal activist Charlie Perkins, observed in an interview that she could not contemplate the prospect of a loss in the referendum for an Indigenous Voice to Parliament. She argued that a loss would be perceived as a vote against Indigenous people—that should the referendum fail, it would be read as rejection. Perkins noted that this

> just might force people to give up, might take them to a point of just shrugging their shoulders and

> turning their back and giving up, and we can't do that. These issues are unfinished business. These are issues that the country must deal with, and a failure of a referendum is just kicking the issue down the road. It is not going to go away.[30]

Criticism also has been levelled at the idea that the referendum is not going to offer a particular model, but rather will ask the Australian voting populace to agree to the principle of an enshrined Voice to Parliament. One of the Voice's chief architects, Professor Megan Davis, argues that the referendum must be about this principle and not the specific model:

> We don't want Australians to vote on a model A and model B … What we want Aussies to vote on is the principle, the fundamental normative principle; should the Commonwealth be talking to blackfellas when it makes laws and policies? … You really cannot design a fully fledged model before you vote, because you do risk enshrining that model in the Constitution.[31]

As a constitutional law expert, Davis notes that the Constitution needs to be concerned with principles, not specificities and model details, which are unnecessary and could even be distracting.

Support for the Voice can be found on both sides of politics. Former Liberal member of the House of Representatives Ken Wyatt is not known for radical politics, but rather is considered to be a modern or moderate Liberal. In 2017, Wyatt was appointed minister for Indigenous Australians, the first Indigenous person to hold the position. But Wyatt resigned from the Liberals in 2023 in protest at the party's opposition to the referendum. In an interview, Wyatt noted the racism underlying this stance and suggested hypocrisy when he observed:

> It was not a challenge when we became multicultural Australia. When we established advisory bodies at state and territory levels for different ethnic communities, it was accepted. We accepted a national body—and yet I did not hear, from my recollection, a swell of backlash from this nation of Australians when we did that.[32]

Thomas Mayo, Kaurareg Aboriginal and Kalkalgal, Erubamle Torres Strait Islander man, is another steadfast campaigner for the Voice to Parliament. As he has pointed out in several interviews and public talks, the referendum is an Aboriginal and Torres Strait Islander idea, not something dreamed into existence by politicians. The referendum will ask voters whether we agree that Indigenous peoples—with over 60 000 years of heritage and culture—are an essential part of our identity as Australians, and if they should be given a fair say in matters relating to them. As Mayo notes: 'Why wouldn't we say "Yes"?'[33]

The perspective of the authors of this book is that, both historically and legally, the Voice is a legitimate, effective and coherent response to the Uluru Statement. It fulfils the requirements of international human rights law by recognising the right to self-determination and the right to free, prior and informed consent of First Nations peoples. It fulfils the goals of the independent work on constitutional recognition leading up to this moment, including the efforts of the Referendum Council, the Indigenous Voice Co-design Process, and the Uluru Dialogues. It is a representative body which maintains the role and powers of the parliament and does not create any veto or other powers. Beyond these rationales, the Voice, and the referendum being held to entrench the body, represent political maturity and social cohesion, as befits a sophisticated nation.

Indigenous peoples' claims are often expressed as calls for a treaty, for sovereignty or for self-determination, to address the fault line initiated by Cook and his successors. These calls should not be dismissed as unfeasible. Our common-law cousins have found their own mechanisms for establishing proper lawful relations with indigenous communities, whether as 'domestic dependent nations', tribes or citizens. These have not caused disruption or interfered with democratic processes.

~

Let us return to the Uluru Statement from the Heart, and the need to embrace 'Voice, Treaty, Truth':

> We call for the establishment of a First Nations Voice enshrined in the Constitution. Makarrata is the culmination of our agenda: the coming together after a struggle. It captures our aspirations for a fair and truthful relationship with the people of Australia and a better future for our children based on justice and self-determination. We seek a Makarrata Commission to supervise a process of agreement-making between governments and First Nations and truth-telling about our history.

> In 1967 we were counted, in 2017 we seek to be heard. We leave base camp and start our trek across this vast country.
>
> We invite you to walk with us in a movement of the Australian people for a better future.

In 2023, Indigenous Australia asks that we listen to their invitation and advocate for the Voice. As described in this book, Australia has been relatively poor at listening. The time to listen is now. As a representative advisory body, the Voice can be understood as an essential part of the national journey to repair the fault line created by law since James Cook first declared British possession of this land. It will embed genuine legal recognition and a relationship between Indigenous communities and peoples and the nation-state. The very point of this recognition is to preclude Indigenous people from being controlled and coerced unilaterally by the state.

Throughout this book, we have shown that sustained, generational attempts have been made by Indigenous Australians to be heard and accounted for. These requests have not been rushed. It has been a long wait, but now is the time to listen, to truly hear, acknowledge and accommodate. The Voice to Parliament shifts the relationship between First

Nations peoples and the state from a monologue to a dialogue, from unilateral to multilateral, from a majoritarian agenda to a consultative and participatory one. This recognition and relationship are not just essential for First Nations but are fundamental to Australia as a constitutional democracy. The referendum to entrench it in the Constitution is unequivocally in the national interest.[34]

ACKNOWLEDGEMENTS

We acknowledge that we work, write and research on the lands of the Wurundjeri and Bunurong people of the Kulin nation. We pay our respects to their Elders past and present, and acknowledge their ongoing right and responsibility to care for Country, lands and waters that were taken and never ceded. Lynette Russell also thanks the Australian Research Council Centre of Excellence for Australian Biodiversity and Heritage for their support. She acknowledges her Monash University colleagues at the Indigenous Studies Centre, particularly the Global Encounters Team and Ian McNiven. Melissa Castan thanks her research collaborators, especially Dr Kate Galloway, who have all generously shared ideas, inquiries and resolutions. She also thanks Robert Lehrer and her colleagues at Monash Law and at the Castan Centre for Human Rights Law for their support and advocacy.

NOTES

1 Information from the Australian Institute of Aboriginal and Torres Strait Islander Studies (AIATSIS), a federal government–funded and sanctioned collection and research agency dedicated to Indigenous Australia. Lynette Russell has been a member of AIATSIS for over twenty years.
2 The full text of the Uluru Statement can be found here: https://ulurustatement.org/the-statement (viewed June 2023).
3 Museum of Australian Democracy, 'Secret Instructions to Lieutenant Cook 30 July 1768 (UK)', https://www.foundingdocs.gov.au/item-did-34.html (viewed June 2023).
4 Richard Broome, *Aboriginal Victorians: A History since 1800*, Allen & Unwin, Crows Nest, NSW, 2005.
5 A great deal has been written on the mission at Coranderrk. For an excellent overview of how Aboriginal people made themselves heard, see Diane Barwick, Richard Essex Barwick and Laura E Barwick, *Rebellion at Coranderrk*, Aboriginal History Inc, Canberra, 1998; and Giordano Nanni and Andrea James, *Coranderrk: We Will Show the Country*, Aboriginal Studies Press, Canberra, 2013.
6 Cumeroogunga was an Aboriginal mission on the New South Wales side of the Murray River. For a comprehensive biography of William Cooper, see Bain Attwood, *William Cooper: An Aboriginal Life Story*, Miegunyah Press, Carlton, Vic., 2021.
7 Marcia Langton and Aaron David Samuel Corn, *Law: The Way of the Ancestors*, Thames & Hudson/National Museum Australia, Port Melbourne, Vic., 2023.
8 High Court of Australia, 'Mabo v Queensland (No 2)

("Mabo case") [1992] HCA 23; (1992) 175 CLR 1 (3 June 1992)', http://www7.austlii.edu.au/cgi-bin/viewdoc/au/cases/cth/HCA/1992/23.html (viewed June 2023).

9 Mark McKenna has written an excellent overview of the media responses and the emergence of the black armband view of history: see Mark McKenna, 'Different Perspectives on Black Armband History', Australian Government, Research Paper No. 5, 1997–98, https://parlinfo.aph.gov.au/parlInfo/download/library/prspub/B5N30/upload_binary/B5N30.pdf;fileType=application%2Fpdf#search=%22library/prspub/B5N30%22 (viewed June 2023).

10 For a detailed exploration of the Intervention's effectiveness, see Stephen Gray, *The Northern Territory Intervention: An Evaluation*, Castan Centre for Human Rights Law, Clayton, Vic., February 2020, https://www.monash.edu/__data/assets/pdf_file/0003/2106156/NT-Intervention-Evaluation-Report-2020.pdf (viewed June 2023).

11 See Closing the Gap, 2023, https://www.closingthegap.gov.au (viewed June 2023).

12 Fiona Stanley and Marcia Langton, 'How the Voice Can Help Close the Gap', in Thomas Mayo and Kerry O'Brien, *The Voice to Parliament Handbook*, Hardie Grant, Melbourne, 2023, pp. 73–80.

13 S James Anaya, *Indigenous Peoples in International Law*, Oxford University Press, New York, 2004, p. 104.

14 United Nations, 'UN Declaration on the Rights of Indigenous Peoples', 13 September 2007, https://www.ohchr.org/en/indigenous-peoples/un-declaration-rights-indigenous-peoples (viewed June 2023).

15 Anaya, *Indigenous Peoples in International Law*, p. 104.

16 UNDRIP, articles 3, 4 and 18.

17 UNDRIP, Article 19.

18 As described, for example, by Shireen Morris, *Radical Heart*, Melbourne University Press, Carlton, Vic., 2018; and Pat Anderson and Megan Davis, *Our Voices from the Heart*, Harper Collins, Sydney, 2023.

19 Referendum Council, *Final Report of the Referendum Council*, 30 June 2017, https://www.referendumcouncil.org.au/sites/default/files/report_attachments/Referendum_Council_Final_Report.pdf (viewed June 2023).

20 Notably, Leeser's commitment to the Voice was such that he stepped away from a leadership role in protest at the Peter Dutton–led opposition to the Voice.
21 Tom Calma and Marcia Langton, *Indigenous Voice Co-design Process: Final Report to the Australian Government*, National Indigenous Australians Agency, July 2021, https://voice.gov.au/resources/indigenous-voice-co-design-process-final-report (viewed June 2023).
22 Ian Anderson, 'There Are No Second Chances in This Voice Referendum', *Financial Review*, 12 April 2023, https://www.afr.com/politics/federal/there-are-no-second-chances-in-this-voice-referendum-20230411-p5czg6 (viewed June 2023).
23 Jarred Cross, '"A Whole Generation of Leadership Will Have Failed" if Voice Defeated—Noel Pearson', National Indigenous Times, 21 February 2023, https://nit.com.au/21-02-2023/5031/a-no-vote-on-the-voice-will-mean-indigenous-leaders-have-failed-says-noel-pearson (viewed June 2023).
24 Lorena Allam, 'If yes campaign for Indigenous voice loses "racists will feel emboldened"', *The Guardian*, 7 April 2023, https://www.theguardian.com/australia-news/2023/apr/07/if-yes-campaign-for-indigenous-voice-loses-racists-will-feel-emboldened-marcia-langton-says (viewed June 2023).
25 Anderson, 'There Are No Second Chances in This Voice Referendum'.
26 Michelle Grattan, 'Grattan on Friday: A "No" Vote in the Voice Referendum Would Put a Serious Dent in Australia's Image Abroad', *The Conversation*, 23 March 2023, https://theconversation.com/grattan-on-friday-a-no-vote-in-the-voice-referendum-would-put-a-serious-dent-in-australias-image-abroad-201157 (viewed June 2023).
27 *ABC News*, 'Linda Burney Says Australia Is the Only First World Nation with a Colonial History that Doesn't Recognise Its First People in Its Constitution. Is She Correct?', 10 October 2019, https://www.abc.net.au/news/2019-10-10/fact-check3a-is-australia-the-only-first-world-nation-with-a-c/11583706 (viewed June 2023).
28 Eddie Synot, 'The Uluru Statement and Changing the Culture of Power and Decision-Making', Indigenous Constitutional

Law, 28 October 2021, https://www.indigconlaw.org/home/the-uluru-statement-and-changing-the-culture-of-power-and-decision-making (viewed June 2023).
29 Josh Butler, 'Noel Pearson Warns of "Almost Endless Protest" if Indigenous Voice Referendum Fails', *The Guardian*, 1 May 2023, https://www.theguardian.com/australia-news/2023/may/01/noel-pearson-warns-of-almost-endless-protest-if-indigenous-voice-referendum-fails (viewed June 2023).
30 Martin McKenzie-Murray, '"Unfinished Business": The People behind the "Yes" Case', *The Saturday Paper*, 29 April 2023, https://www.thesaturdaypaper.com.au/news/politics/2023/04/29/unfinished-business-the-people-behind-the-yes-case#hrd (viewed June 2023).
31 Tom McIlroy, 'The High-stakes Gamble at the Heart of the Voice', *Financial Review*, 28 April 2023, https://www.afr.com/politics/federal/the-high-stakes-gamble-at-the-heart-of-the-voice-20230317-p5ct3g (viewed June 2023).
32 Lorena Allam, 'Dysfunctional Treatment of Indigenous Australians Will Continue Unless Voice Exists, Ken Wyatt Says', *The Guardian*, 28 April 2023, https://www.theguardian.com/australia-news/2023/apr/28/dysfunctional-treatment-of-indigenous-australians-will-continue-unless-voice-exists-ken-wyatt-says (viewed June 2023).
33 Thomas Mayo, 'Voice Myths Debunked: Thomas Mayo', *The Geraldton Guardian*, 13 May 2023.
34 Melissa Castan, 'Constitutional Recognition, Self-Determination and an Indigenous Representative Body', *Indigenous Law Bulletin*, vol. 8, no. 19, 2015, p. 15.

IN THE NATIONAL INTEREST

Other books on the issues that matter:

David Anderson *Now More than Ever: Australia's ABC*
Bill Bowtell *Unmasked: The Politics of Pandemics*
Michael Bradley *System Failure: The Silencing of Rape Survivors*
Inala Cooper *Marrul: Aboriginal Identity & the Fight for Rights*
Samantha Crompvoets *Blood Lust, Trust & Blame*
Satyajit Das *Fortune's Fool: Australia's Choices*
Richard Denniss *Big: The Role of the State in the Modern Economy*
Rachel Doyle *Power & Consent*
Jo Dyer *Burning Down the House: Reconstructing Modern Politics*
Wayne Errington & Peter van Onselen *Who Dares Loses: Pariah Policies*
Gareth Evans *Good International Citizenship: The Case for Decency*
Kate Fitz-Gibbon *Our National Shame: Violence against Women*
Paul Fletcher *Governing in the Internet Age*
Carrillo Gantner *Dismal Diplomacy, Disposable Sovereignty: Our Problem with China & America*
Jill Hennessy *Respect*
Lucinda Holdforth *21st-Century Virtues: How They Are Failing Our Democracy*
Simon Holmes à Court *The Big Teal*
Andrew Leigh *Fair Game: Lessons from Sport for a Fairer Society & a Stronger Economy*
Ian Lowe *Australia on the Brink: Avoiding Environmental Ruin*
John Lyons *Dateline Jerusalem: Journalism's Toughest Assignment*
Richard Marles *Tides that Bind: Australia in the Pacific*
Fiona McLeod *Easy Lies & Influence*
Michael Mintrom *Advancing Human Rights*
Louise Newman *Rape Culture*
Martin Parkinson *A Decade of Drift*
Abul Rizvi *Population Shock*
Kevin Rudd *The Case for Courage*
Don Russell *Leadership*
Scott Ryan *Challenging Politics*
Kate Thwaites & Jenny Macklin *Enough Is Enough*
Simon Wilkie *The Digital Revolution: A Survival Guide*
Campbell Wilson *Living with AI*